Happiness in Living Color

Inspiration by Ieda Jónasdóttir Herman
Compiled by Heidi Herman

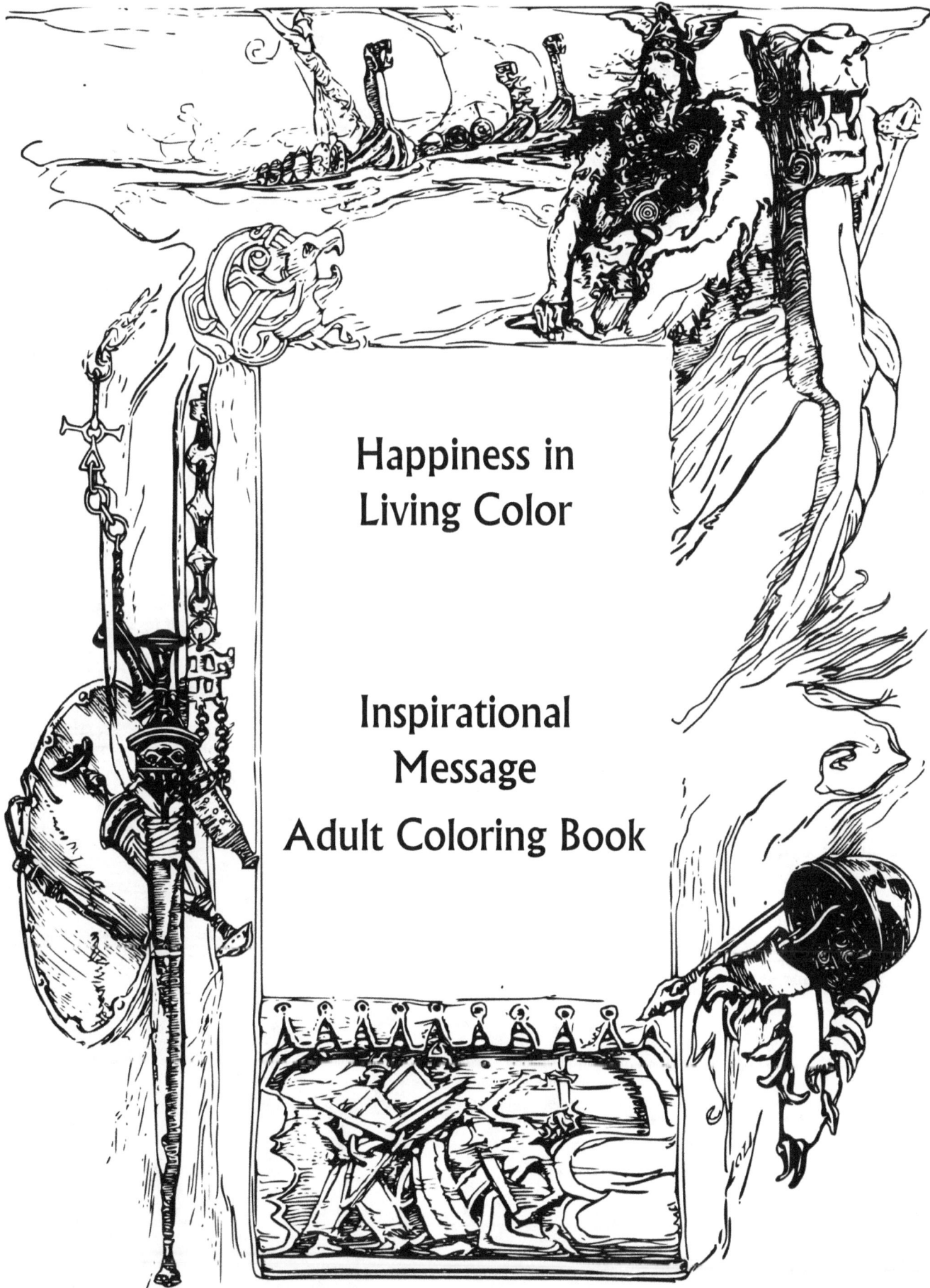

Happiness in
Living Color

Inspirational
Message
Adult Coloring Book

Hekla Publishing LLC
Color Me Happy
Adult Coloring Book
ISBN: 978-1-947233-95-9

Ieda Jónasdóttir Herman is an Icelandic-born life explorer who inspires many through her vitality, positive attitude, and endless energy.

To those around her, she is known as Viking Amma

These inspirational thoughts and motivational ideas are her foundation for a happy life. May they inspire you as well.

I always try to get a window seat when flying on an airplane. I love to look down on the earth from the angels point of view

My Grandfather's early training and admonition that "Viking kids don't cry" has helped me to have courage and a strong will

Some call it foolhardy and stubborn but it has served me well

We can't live like
chickens in a coop
and expect to be
able to soar the
skies like seagulls

I do have a choice
when I wake up in the
morning.

I can think about the
aches and pains;
about the troubles of
the day....OR, I can
choose to be happy.

I choose to be happy.

This is the day The Lord has made,
I WILL rejoice and be glad in it.
-Psalm 118:24

HONEY

DARLING

MY

LOVE

SWEETHEART

The Bold and

The Generous

Have

The Best Lives

-Icelandic Proverb

Never Stop Moving.

It seems the more I move, the more energy I have.

I wait on the microwave to finish and do a little dance. Whether I feel like it or not, I always seem to smile when I dance.

Then I have energy and I'm happy too! I think they call that a win-win!

When I need to think, I
head for water.

A lake, a river, a little
pond.

There's something about
the water that is peaceful.

Attitude is Everything
Choose to believe

Yes I can ~ Yes you can ~
Yes we can.

Choose a different perspective
to change how you see things

The word "No"
turned upside-down
becomes "On"

I Aspire To Inspire Before I Expire

Be someone's inspiration

I am far to busy enjoying
life to be limited by
acting my age.

Whatever that means.

Join my adventure or be
content to watch ~

Just don't tell me I can't
follow my dreams.

Find the Good

The world is filled with heartache, pain, and sadness. There are plenty of mean people, anger, selfishness, and unhappiness.

There is also light, life, and laughter. There are beautiful views everywhere around you if you choose to look and see.

There are also good people. People who care and help others.

If you have trouble finding one, make sure you are one.

The people around you need it.

Whatever there is to do

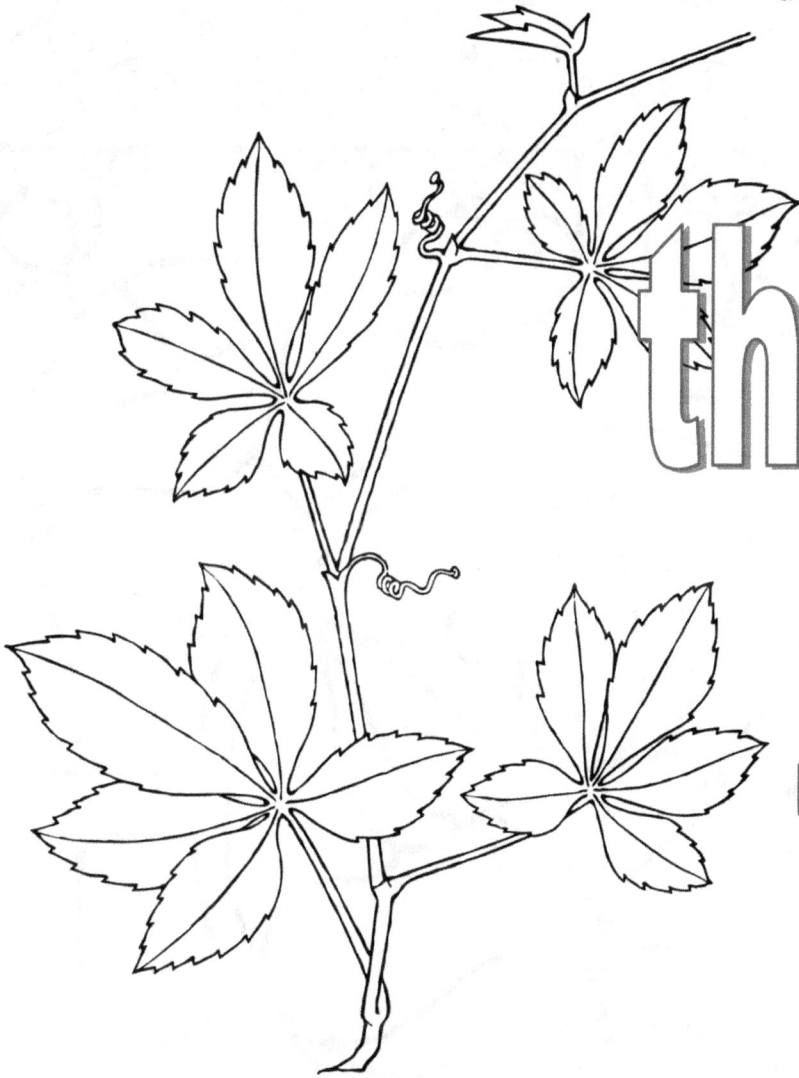

Do that thing

Grow where
You are
Planted

SHARE YOUR SMILE

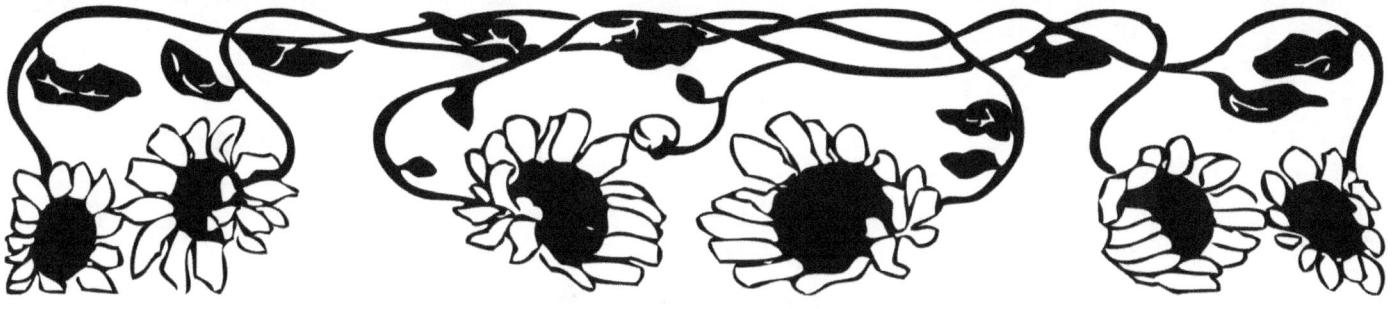

"Much always longs for more"
-Icelandic Proverb

I have always found I am happiest with what I have when I don't compare it to what others have.

I don't have to keep up with the Jones'—I've taken a different road.

The sun shines every day.

Just because sometimes it's covered with clouds doesn't mean it's not still there

Dance

Between

the

Raindrops

Friends are sometimes like

butterflies that

come into your

life and leave

too quickly.

Love them
while they
are with you.

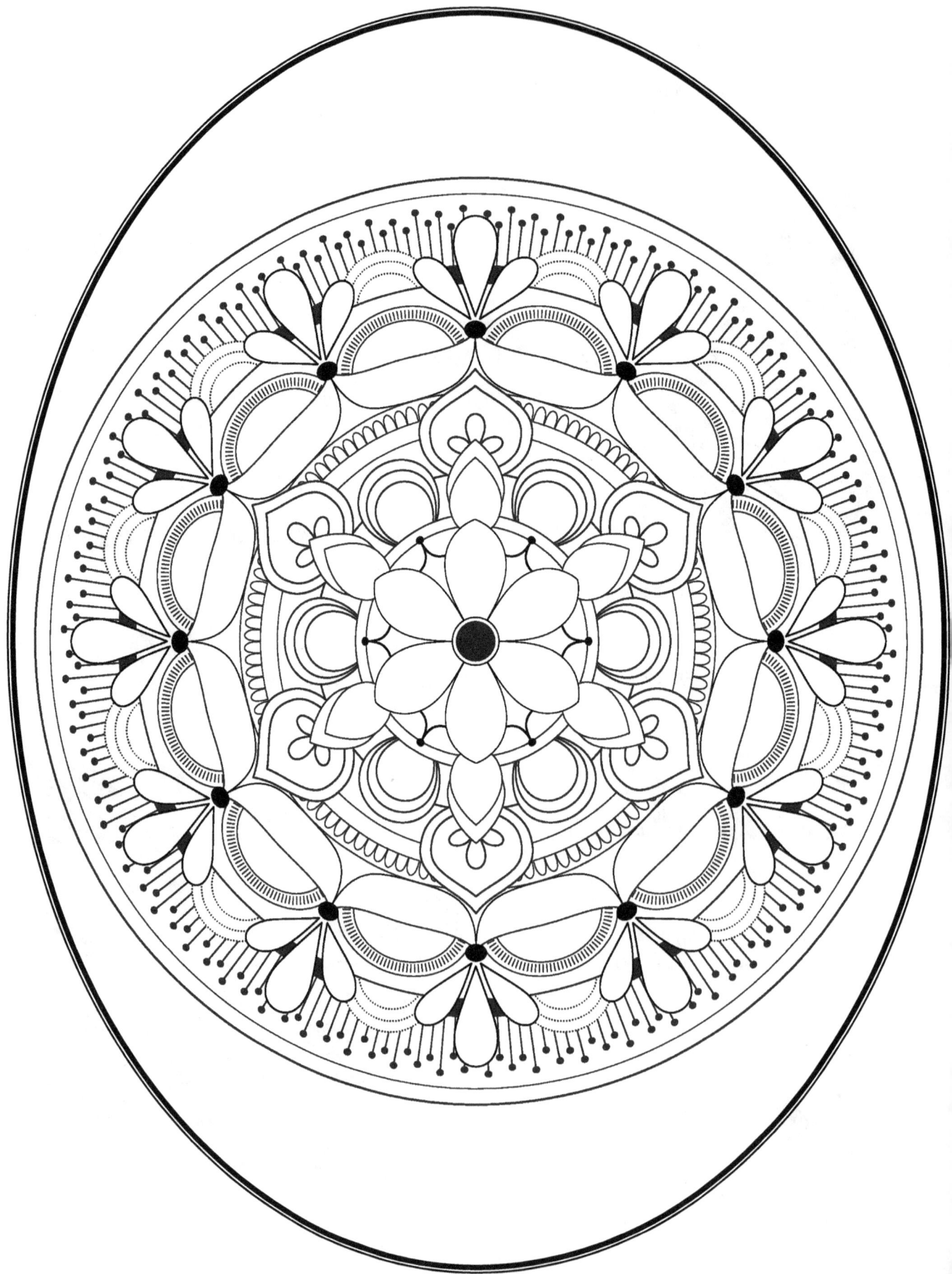

Yesterday cannot be re-lived and regret
serves no purpose

Tomorrow isn't here yet and worry won't
solve any problems.

Today is all you have. Live in the moment.
Treasure it and make the most of it.

You are not guaranteed that tomorrow will
come. If it doesn't, know that you gave your
best today.

Be happy, be vibrant. Love yourself and
those around you.

Today is the best day to be alive.

LOVE
WITHOUT
LIMITS

Wine & Chocolate

My doctor told me I needed more greens in my diet. On the way home, I stopped and bought my favorite candy-coated chocolate.

Thank goodness there were green ones in there.

Another doctor told me Muscatine grapes were good for me. So, I bought the convenient liquid form.

Who am I to question doctor's orders?

I kept seeing a lot of articles about Yoga and I became interested and added it to my routine. I didn't care that I was over 80. Nothing I read said I shouldn't.

I wanted to share my memories of growing up in Iceland. I wrote my childhood memoirs when I was 85. Nobody told me I couldn't.

I always wanted to fly like the seagulls in Iceland. At 88, my wish came true when I was given the opportunity to go paragliding in Utah. I never once thought I wouldn't.

I should

I can

I will

Every dream is within my power to achieve.

I love reading the insights and thoughts of great minds.

I am so inspired by the writings of Thomas Jefferson, Benjamin Franklin, Eleanor Roosevelt, Winston Churchill, and Thomas Edison.

Who inspires you?

If the way I have lived my life has instilled in my children a zest for life, a thirst for knowledge, and a desire to experience all the world has to offer, then I have done well.

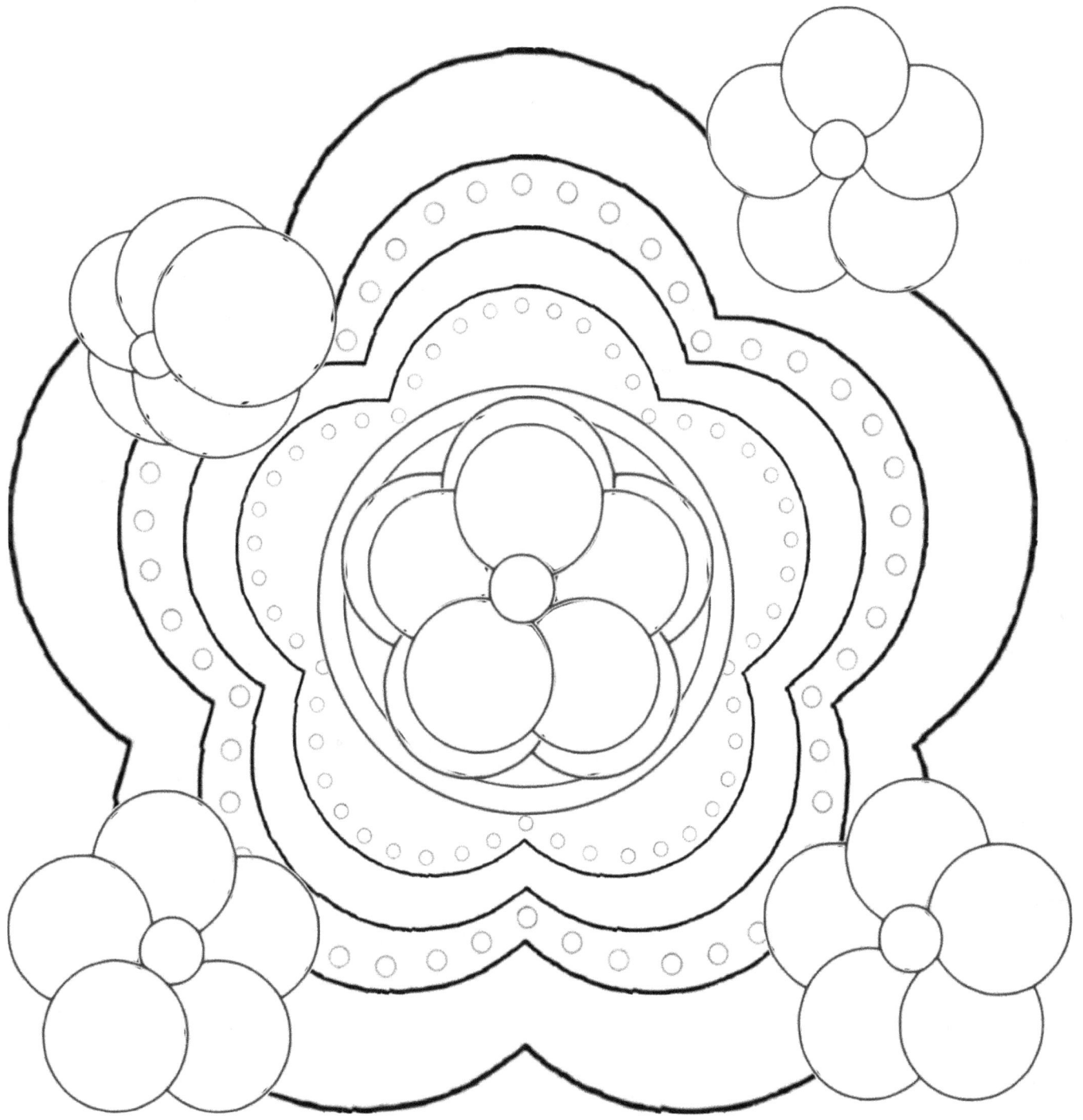

www.ingramcontent.com/pod-product-compliance
Lightning Source LLC
Chambersburg PA
CBHW081230020426
42331CB00012B/3109